YOUR KNOWLEDGE HAS VALUE

The Development of Ticket Prices in German Professional Soccer. Dynamic Pricing in Soccer

Nils Sifrin

Bibliographic information published by the German National Library:

The German National Library lists this publication in the National Bibliography; detailed bibliographic data are available on the Internet at http://dnb.dnb.de.

ISBN: 9783346284945
This book is also available as an ebook.

Faculty of Business Administration and Economics
Chair of Organizational, Media and Sports Economics

Bachelor Thesis

Ticket Prices in German Professional Soccer

due date:

17.07.2017

submitted by:

Nils Sifrin

Executive Summary

All professional sports team are effectively a business, and these sports teams focus on two goals: Performance on the field and performance off the field. Performance on the field is a factor on relative business success; however this Bachelor Thesis will examine the effect of the Dynamic pricing. In other words, how performance on the field affects performance off the field for professional German soccer teams, and vice-versa. The strategy for adequate performance off the field requires maximizing the revenue of ticket sales, and maximizing the degree of capacity utilization. This thesis will advance the viability of using Dynamic Pricing for the contemporary environment of German professional soccer teams. Expanded, this includes the viability it has when applying to the hotel and tourism environments. For comparison, Dynamic Pricing has been used in the United States, and this thesis will examine the effect of the strategy on United States' professional sports. While risks associated with using this strategy are presented, this thesis works to address each of these issues, and provide insight on how this strategy can still find success in separately, the First Bundesliga and the Second Bundesliga. This thesis will show evidence concluding that Dynamic Pricing will be able to solve the goals of maximizing revenue and maximizing capacity utilization by putting their fans first. Through thoughtful analysis of the German Club's fans, Dynamic Pricing can aid teams and fans to flourish alongside each other.

Table of Contents

List of figures

List of tables

1 Introduction and Motivation

Nowadays in professional sports, clubs are forced to focus on much more than just the sport itself. The clubs in the European top leagues function on the same level to international companies. Bayern Munich, for example, had a turnover of 626.8 million Euro in 2015/2016 season (Statista, 2017). Due to rising salaries for the players and increasing costs in general, clubs are challenged to retain a certain income in order to stay financially and athletically competitive. "With increasing operating costs resulting from rising player salaries and lavish sport-specific facilities, sport managers have been forced to search for additional revenue streams" (Shapiro, S.; Drayer, J.; 2012: p. 532). Aside from advertising revenues and sponsorships, the tickets to the stadium are a regular source of income, as matches generally take place at least once a week. During an average game day over 700,000 people visit the stadiums across the first German soccer league (First Bundesliga). Statistics show that stadiums are often sold out or the number of visitors, on average, is close to the capacity of the stadium. In Season 2016/17 out of 801,872 available seats to first league stadiums on average 747,486 are filled (Transfermarkt, 2017). Additional information reveals that this degree of capacity utilization cannot be replicated in the second German league. Only 391,446 out of 605,896 available seats are filled on an average game day. This means that only 64.61% of the tickets are sold. That being said, some clubs are able to sell nearly all of their tickets whereas some clubs can only fill less than half of their stadium. FC St. Pauli could fill up their stadium to a degree of 99.05% as an average during the season 2016/2017, whereas other clubs like Karlsruher SC and Fortuna Düsseldorf could not break the 50.00% for the same season (Transfermarkt, 2017a). Moreover, Germany's second league performs better in selling tickets to the games than other top leagues across Europe:

Table 1: Degree of Capacity Utilization 2016/17

Country	Number of Available Seats	Number of Average Visitors	Degree of Capacity Utilization
England (Premier League)	750282	716100	95.44%
Germany (1. Bundesliga)	801872	747486	93.22%
Spain (LaLiga)	770302	563060	73.10%
France (Ligue 1)	648957	421600	64.97%
Germany (2. Bundesliga)	605896	391446	64.61%
Italy (Serie A)	806685	440140	54.56%

Source: Based on Transfermarkt.de 2016/17.

The Second Bundesliga has nearly as many available seats as the Ligue 1 in France. The degree of capacity utilization of the second German League is with approximately 65% also as high as in the French first league. With less seats available than in the First Bundesliga, England's Premier League can achieve the highest degree of capacity utilization. It is slightly ahead of the First Bundesliga, but these two leagues get with 95.22% and 93.22% a percentage that is over 20% higher than all other leagues. The Spanish first League, with 73.10%, is in between of Premier League, next First Bundesliga and Ligue 1, and then Second Bundesliga. The Serie A has more available seats, but it cannot fill the stadiums so that the degree of capacity utilization is as low as only 54.56%. This means that in Italy's top league only slightly more than half of the stadium is filled with visitors on average.

The First and the Second Bundesliga consist of eighteen clubs each. All other leagues mentioned above consist of twenty clubs each. It should be easier to divide fans among lesser teams so that it is easier to gain a higher degree of capacity utilization.

Soccer generates numerous fans in Germany who visit their club's stadium regularly, and spend money on more than just a ticket during their visits (Drayer, J.; Shapiro, S.; Lee, S.; 2012: p. 188). Food, drinks, and merchandise are a great source of revenue for clubs. "In sports and any other industry, knowing how to satisfy your customers and give them a better experience will bring additional dollars to the organization" (Castro Jr., S. M., 2014: p. 3). Filling up the stadiums will activate these multiplier effects.

Thus, besides winning games, management should focus on two things in regard to their customer base:

1. *Maximizing the revenue of the ticket sale*

2. *Maximizing the degree of capacity utilization*

Clubs should consider different pricing strategies to optimize their ticket revenue. Most seem to define their ticket pricing during the preseason. However, this leaves little room for other factors, such as athletic performance over the course of the season that cannot be taken into consideration. In conclusion, clubs are not currently flexible with their pricing strategy. Dynamic Pricing could be "the future of ticket pricing in sports" (Rishe, P., 2012: p. 1).

Can dynamic pricing help to realize the two aforementioned goals?

This Bachelor Thesis will examine the development of ticket prices in German professional soccer. The data gathered from the first and second divisions will be compared to current prices in other European leagues as well as other sports to determine if clubs should charge more money for tickets.

Furthermore, this thesis will discuss the viability of dynamic pricing strategies in German professional soccer. Therefore, dynamic pricing in the hotel and tourism sector will be adapted to the current situation at German professional soccer. Advantages and disadvantages of dynamic pricing will be analyzed to optimize pricing strategies for German soccer clubs. These recommendations will be separately projected on the First and the Second Bundesliga.

2 Ticket Prices in the Professional Team Sport Industry

For the empirical part of this thesis, the ticket fees from the first and second German soccer leagues were analyzed. The time frame that was observed spans the last ten seasons, from 2007/2008 to 2016/2017. Ticket prices are categorized in four different tiers: First and second tier are the most expensive, and the cheapest, tickets for seats. Third and fourth tier are the most expensive, and the cheapest, tickets for standing room only. The following graphics below show the average ticket prices of every club for each tier group of every season.

2.1 Ticket Prices in German Soccer

Figure 1: Price development in the First Bundesliga 1st Tier

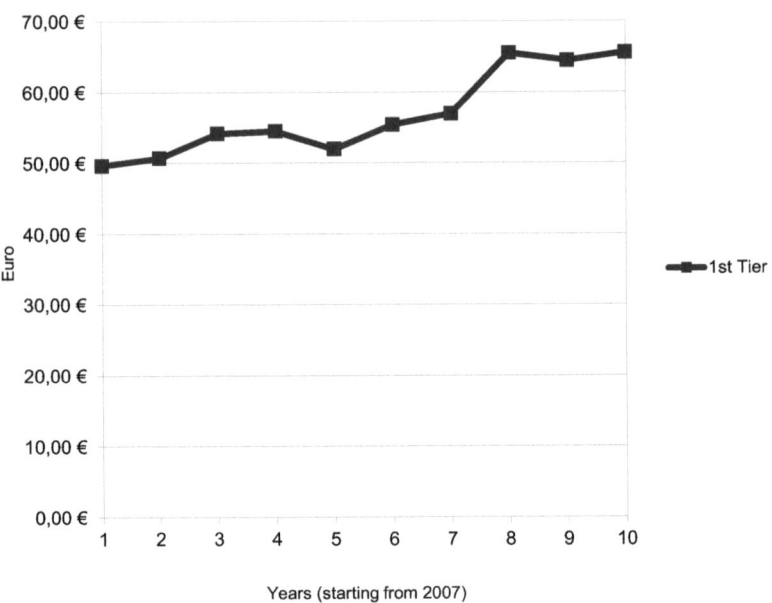

Source: Based on Sportbild Sonderhefte Bundesliga 2007/08 – 2016/17.

Figure 2: Price development in the First Bundesliga 2nd Tier, 3rd Tier & 4th Tier

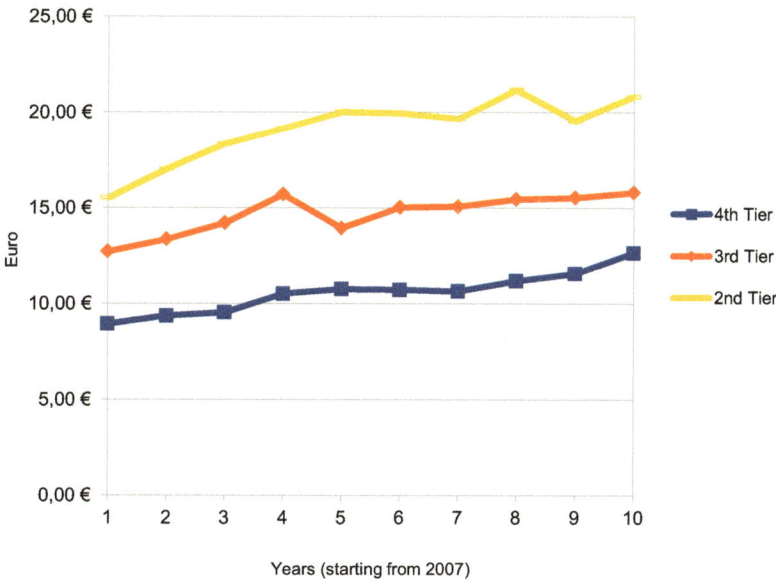

Source: Based on Sportbild Sonderhefte Bundesliga 2007/08 – 2016/17.

Statistically, a rise in price was seen among every different tier of observed tickets. However, there was a dramatic increase in price for top tier seating. In 2007, the average top tier ticket price was 49.64€. Whereas in 2016, one had to pay an average of 65.56€ for a ticket in the same price group.

The rise in price for the other three categories was steady, and went up approximately 4€ within these past ten seasons. Due to the differing increase between the average top tier tickets and the remaining three tiers, the gap between these average prices rose from approximately 35€ in 2007, to 45€ in 2016. Clubs seem to want to charge their wealthiest guests more money, but still keep their average fans coming to the stadium. When dynamic pricing is analyzed later, this aspect will be further discussed.

In the first, second and third tier, top clubs like Bayern Munich and Borussia Dortmund are setting low prices compared to other leagues in Europe. These clubs are giving the tenor concerning the prices of the other clubs. Fans will not accept much higher prices than to stadiums of the top clubs. Thus, clubs like Bayern Munich can dictate the maximum prices for these three tiers. These top clubs have bigger revenue besides their ticket revenue. This is because of better sponsorship, more advertising revenue and so on. This means that they do not depend on the ticket revenue as much as the smaller clubs in the league. By keeping the prices on a lower level, they can control the smaller clubs and discriminate against them. This is because these smaller clubs cannot ask for higher prices. However, the data shows that this does not apply for the first tier tickets. In 2016, Borussia Dortmund prices first tier tickets with 54.40€. Only four teams are pricing their tickets for the first tier cheaper, whereas Bayern Munich is on fifth place together with VFL Wolfsburg, Werder Bremen and TSG Hoffenheim all asking for 70€.

If clubs like Bayern Munich and Borussia Dortmund would higher the ticket prices on a level comparing to other European leagues, smaller clubs could also ask for more money to their stadiums. Their fans would accept higher prices easier if these prices are comparable to the prices of the top clubs within the league.

In general, the clubs in the First German league can be considered as rivals who want to gain many fans. Especially, the geographic location of a club can win fans that live nearby the stadium. However, if more clubs are located in the same area, it might be more difficult to sell tickets for the games. The following map shows the clubs of the First Bundesliga in 2016/2017 season:

Figure 3: Different areas of clubs´ locations of the First Bundesliga

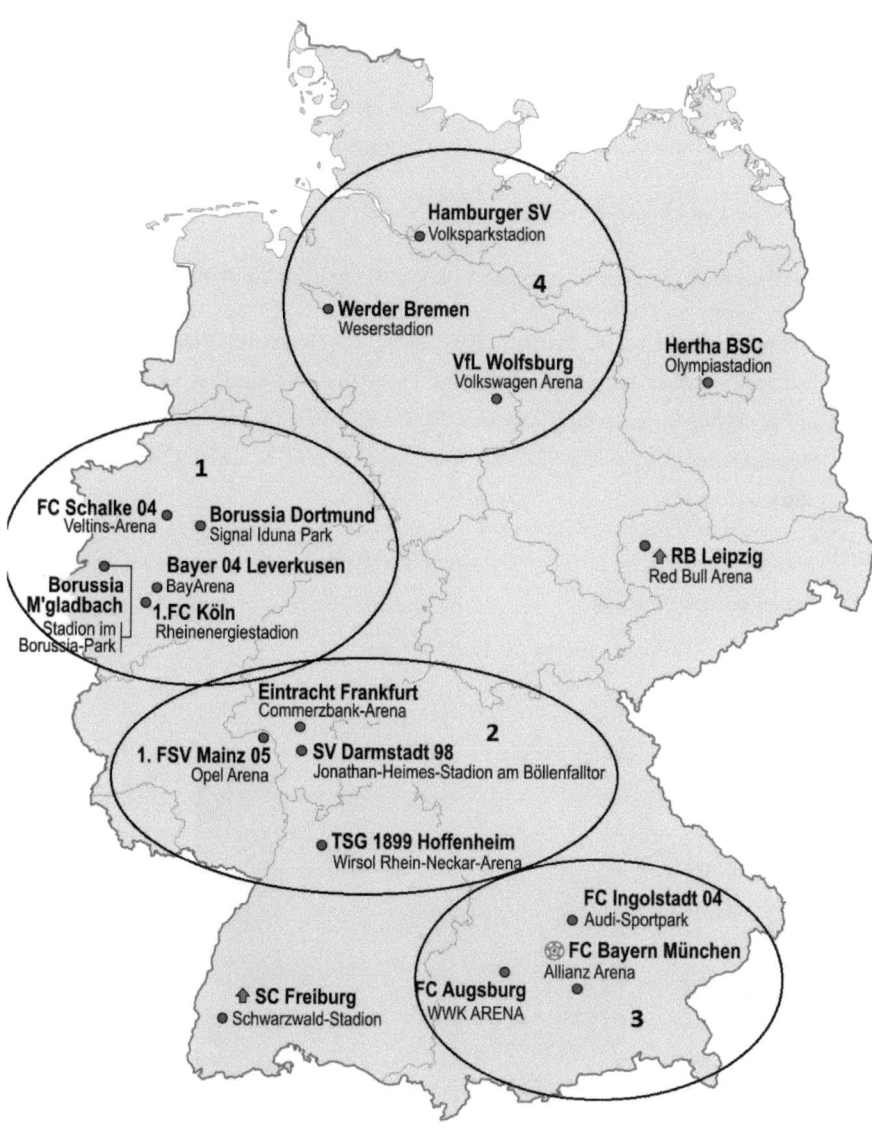

Source: Based on Wikipedia, 2017.

The highest concentration of clubs can be found in the Ruhr area (1). Five big clubs, FC Schalke 04, Borussia Dortmund, Bayer 04 Leverkusen, 1. FC Köln and Borussia Mönchengladbach, are located within a radius of less than a hundred kilometers.

The second area, which is not far away from the first area, consists of Eintracht Frankfurt, FSV Mainz. Darmstadt 98 and TSG 1899 Hoffenheim.

The third area includes Bayern Munich, FC Augsburg and Ingolstadt in South Germany.

Hamburger SV, Werder Bremen and VFL Wolfsburg build the area in North Germany (4).

The remaining clubs, SC Freiburg, RB Leipzig and Hertha BSC, are located by themselves and have a greater distance to other clubs. Especially RB Leipzig is located in East Germany as the only club representing this area. Hertha BSC is with a distance of 190 kilometers the closest club to RB Leipzig. The second closest club, VFL Wolfsburg, is over 200 kilometers away.

The collected data for 2016/2017 season was classified in these categories and the following figures present the results:

Figure 4: Ticket prices in areas 1st Tier First Bundesliga

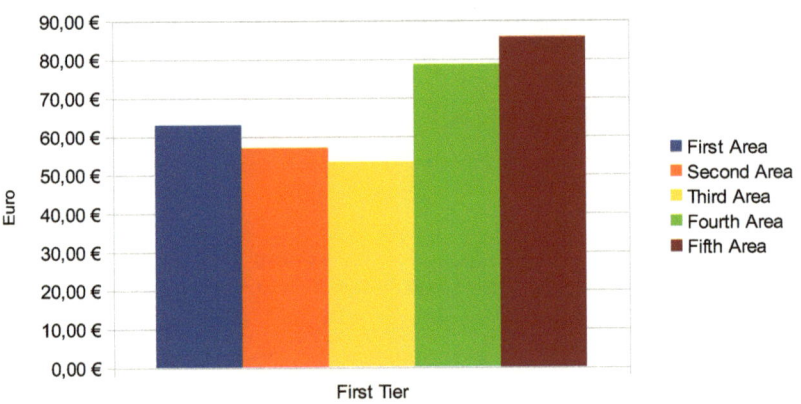

Source: Based on Sportbild Sonderhefte Bundesliga 2007/08 – 2016/17.

Figure 5: Ticket prices in areas 2nd Tier, 3rd Tier & 4th Tier First Bundesliga

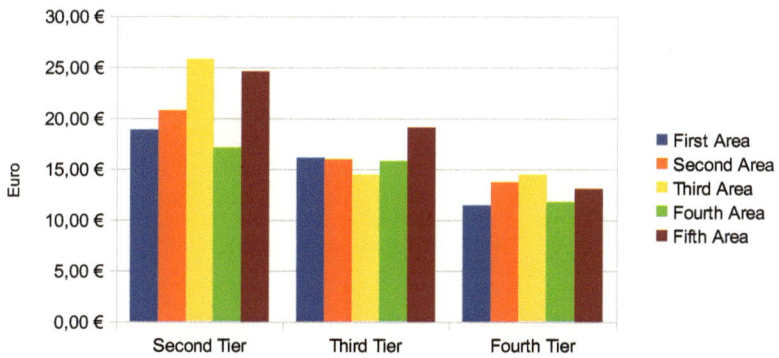

Source: Based on Sportbild Sonderhefte Bundesliga 2007/08 – 2016/17.

The figures show that the clubs of the fifth area, that have no other clubs nearby their location, can ask for higher prices. RB Leipzig categorizes the ticket prices depending on the opponent they have to face. Therefore, their prices are not included in the statistics. Regardless, Hertha BSC, and SC Freiburg demand higher prices for first and third tier tickets than all other areas. In the first tier tickets cost 85.50€ for Hertha BSC Berlin and SC Freiburg, and for example, under 60.00€ for areas 2 and 3. In the third tier, prices compare 19€ (area 5) to approximately 14€ to 16€ in other areas.

In the second tier these clubs demand a much higher price (24.50€) than areas 1, 2 and 4 (17€ to 20€), but lower prices than area 3 (25.67€), consisting of Bayern Munich, FC Augsburg and FC Ingolstadt. In the fourth tier, the cheapest tickets to the stadium, all areas are close together and the prices range from 11.38€ to 14.33€.

Finally, clubs without any nearby rivals can ask for higher prices for tickets.

The following figures present the Second Bundesliga which development in ticket prices will be analyzed in the next paragraph:

Figure 6: Price development in the Second Bundesliga 1st Tier

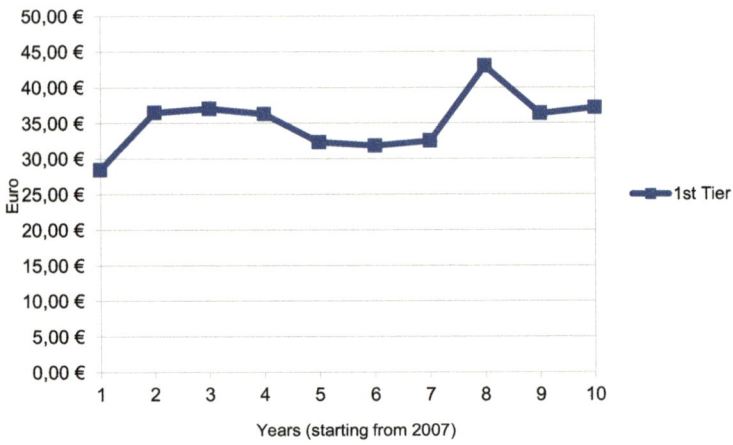

Source: Based on Sportbild Sonderhefte Bundesliga 2007/08 – 2016/17.

Figure 7: Price development in the Second Bundesliga 2nd Tier, 3rd Tier & 4th Tier

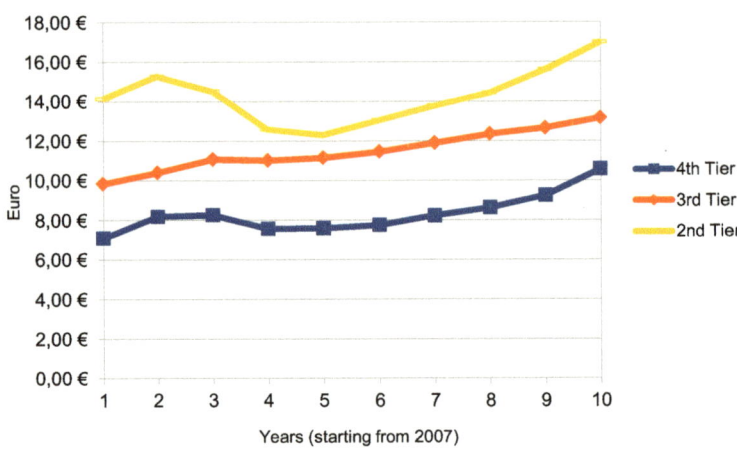

Source: Based on Sportbild Sonderhefte Bundesliga 2007/08 – 2016/17.

The average ticket prices for a second league game show the same tendencies. A small increase was recorded in the three lower tiers and a large increase among the top tier seats. In general, the average rise in ticket price was about half as high as in the First league. On game day, fans must pay about 8€ more for the top tier seats, and additional 2€ for the other categories. The most expensively priced seats are on average 28€ cheaper in the second league, than in the first league. The remaining ticket groups are only about 2€ to 4€ cheaper.

People might not be willing to pay these higher prices for a Second league game, and prefer to visit a first league game in seats of equal coast that is nearby their place of residence. First tier tickets in season 2014/2015 are especially high because FC Heidenheim sold these tickets for 200€. Without this outlier, the graph would show a steady increase from 2013 to 2016. Even though tickets to the second league are significantly cheaper than to the first league, stadiums have a lower turnout (compared in the Introduction). A possible explanation for this is that German second league stadiums have nearly the same capacity than other European top leagues.

Table 2: Average Size of Stadium by Country

Country	Average Size of the Stadium
Germany (1. Bundesliga)	44548
Italy (Serie A)	40334
Spain (LaLiga)	38515
England (Premier League)	37514
Germany (2. Bundesliga)	33660
France (Ligue 1)	32448

Source: Based on Transfermarkt, 2016/17.

The average stadium in the Second Bundesliga offers slightly more seats than the average in Ligue 1 (France). The biggest stadiums, on average, can be found in the First Bundesliga and in Serie A (Italy). However, the degree of capacity utilization compares 93.22% to just 54.56%. Italy seems to have the biggest problem to fill their stadiums across Europe. "Some stadiums have failed to renovate since the World Cup 1990 and the poor conditions have failed to attract fans" (Kelly, D., 2016: p. 1). Opposite to Italy, "in the Bundesliga season 2011/2012, 8 out of 18 clubs play in stadiums that opened their gates for the first time in the new millennium" (Nufer, G.; Fischer, J., 2013: p. 50). Besides old stadiums, the Series A is aired on television for free. "Anyone can basically stay in the comfort of their own home and watch their favorite team" (Kelly, D., 2016: p. 1). This is said to help other European leagues where soccer is not aired on television for free. Empty stadiums lead to "a match atmosphere that has less electricity than an EA Sports video game" (Henderson, J., 2016: p. 1). Empty stadiums mean missing revenue of ticket sales, missing revenue of cross-selling products at the stadium, and failing to bind fans to the club. It also means that playing for this club is less attractive to top players who prefer playing for a club with a crowded stadium every home game.

The clubs in the Second Bundesliga can also be categorized into different areas (2016/2017 season):

Figure 8: Different areas of clubs´ locations of the Second Bundesliga

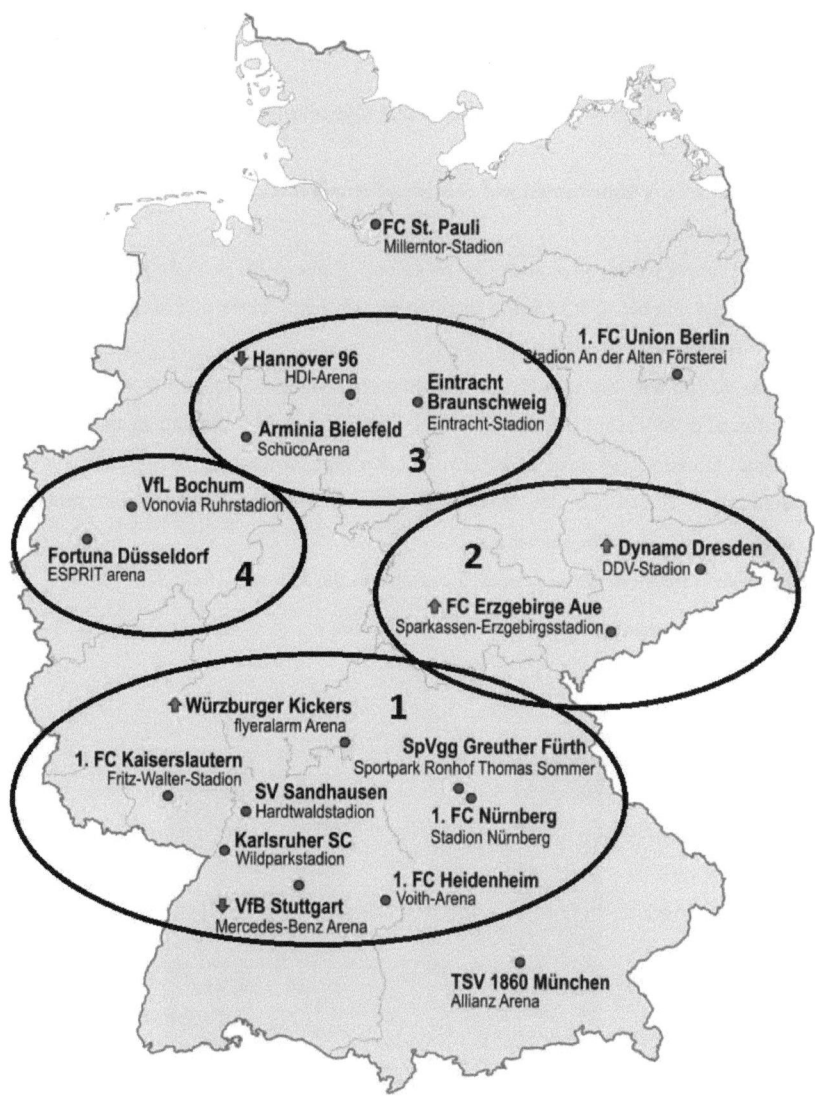

Source: Based on Wikipedia, 2017a.

Area 1 contains most of the teams of the Second Bundesliga: Würzburger Kickers, 1. FC Kaiserslautern, SV Sandhausen, Karlsruher SC, VFB Stuttgart, 1. FC Heidenheim, 1. FC Nürnberg, and SpVgg Greuther Fürth. This means that 8 out of 18 clubs are located in a radius of around 300 kilometers.

The second area is in East Germany, where Dynamo Dresden and FC Erzgebirge Aue are located.

The third area is quite central and consists of Arminia Bielefeld, Hannover 96, and Eintracht Braunschweig.

The Ruhr area has also two teams in the second league. VFL Bochum and Fortuna Düsseldorf are in area number 4. It is worth mentioning that many clubs of this area are playing in the First Bundesliga.

Clubs that do not have close rivals are categorized in area 5 again. FC St. Pauli, 1. FC Union Berlin, and TSV 1860 Munich have no opponents nearby playing in the Second German league. However, all three clubs have another club in the same city who plays in the first Bundesliga. Hamburger SV, Hertha BSC Berlin, and Bayern Munich are representing the same locations in the higher league.

The results for these different areas are shown in the following figures:

Figure 9: Ticket prices in areas 1st Tier Second Bundesliga

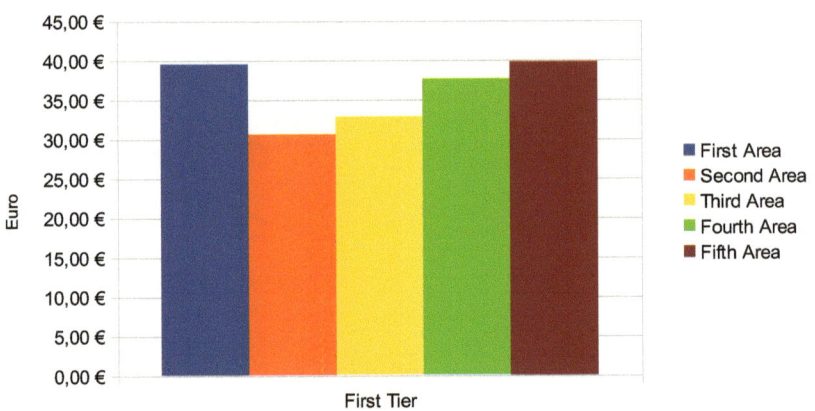

Source: Based on Sportbild Sonderhefte Bundesliga 2007/08 – 2016/17.

Figure 10: Ticket prices in areas 2nd Tier, 3rd Tier & 4th Tier Second Bundesliga

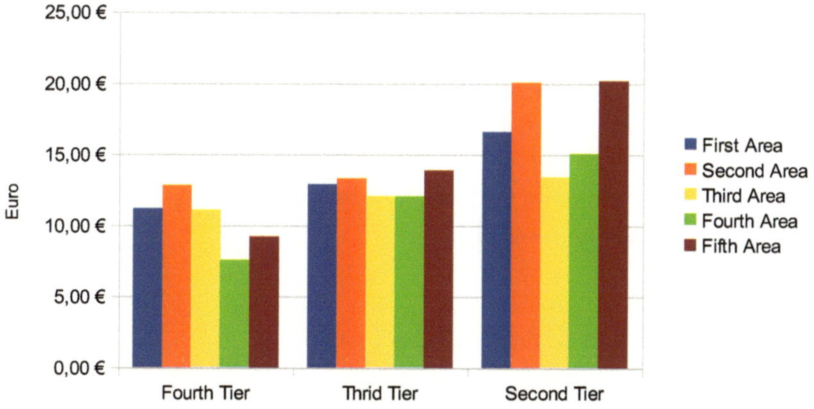

Source: Based on Sportbild Sonderhefte Bundesliga 2007/08 – 2016/17.

Analyzing the figures show mixed results. Clubs without any other clubs nearby have the highest ticket prices for first, second and third tier, but the differences in prices are marginal in the Second Bundesliga. For the cheaper seats (second tier) area 2 and area 5 are around 20€, whereas other areas are only around approximately 15€.

To conclude, these mixed results show that having a location far away from rivals does not matter as much as in the First Bundesliga.

2.2   Ticket Prices in other European Soccer Leagues

"The Premier League has been criticized for the high prices by supporters´ groups" (Un-known., 2013: p. 1). The presented data above confirms this statement: The cheapest average ticket price for the Bundesliga is around 10€. Whereas one is forced to pay nearly three times this amount in the Premier League. "The Bundesliga does a better job of combining competi-tiveness with accessibility" (Unknown, 2013: p. 1). This statement is true compared to the other major leagues across Europe as well. The cheapest game day ticket for La Liga (Spain) is around 28€. For the Serie A (Italy) is around 17€. Clubs in Spain and Great Britain are "at risk of pricing out some sections of its fanbase" (Unknown. 2013: p. 1). It could prove costly to clubs, that young people cannot afford tickets so that '"future generations might be lost" (Unknown., 2013: p. 1) to the game after a Guardian survey revealed.

Although many people criticized the prices in the Premier League this season, stadiums were filled between 97.5% and 99.4% (Soccerstats, 2017). "In fact, it is the second highest average attendance across all sports leagues worldwide behind the National Football League (NFL)" (Nufer, G.; Fischer, J., 2013: p. 50).

This leads to the conclusion that people are willing to pay higher prices for tickets than German clubs are charging nowadays.

2.3   Ticket Prices in the US Major Leagues

Ticket prices in the USA are higher than in Europe. Not only does the U.S. host the third expensive sporting event in the world, the Super Bowl, but regular season NFL games cost more than any soccer games in any European country. In 2013, the average ticket for the Super Bowl cost 1,210$, but "third party ticket prices were listed as high as 316,000$" (Michaels, C., 2017: p. 1). Only the Grand Prix in Abu Dhabi and the 2013 PGA Golf Masters were more expensive. In 2016, the average NFL ticket prices at nearly 93$ (Statista, 2017a).

The MLS, even though soccer is not that popular in the US, has higher ticket prices than the Bundesliga, or than the Ligue 1. A ticket to a game at the MLS costs an average of around 42€. The MLS tries to enhance the attractiveness of the league by signing famous players from Europe. For example, paying a good salary to older players, like Bastian Schweinsteiger and Andre Pirlo. These are just two examples who moved to play in the United States (Willens, M., 2015).

Besides charging higher prices, it is noteworthy that some American sport clubs started using Dynamic Pricing. "In 2009, the San Francisco Giants, a Major League Baseball (MLB) team, became the first sports team to implement a dynamic ticket pricing system, similar to revenue management systems used by airlines and hotels" (Nufer, G.; Fischer, J., 2013: p. 56). In 2015 "at least one-quarter of NFL teams are using dynamic ticket pricing" (Kaplan, D., 2015). As a conclusion, "dynamic pricing is on the edge of becoming an industry standard in US sports" (Nufer, G.; Fischer, J., 2013: p. 59). The San Francisco Giants were able to increase their ticket revenue by 7% in 2010 (Drayer, J.; Shapiro, S.; Lee, S., 2012: p. 185). However, "more empirical evidence is needed to understand these pricing strategies within the context of sporting events" (Shapiro, S.; Drayer, J.; 2012: p. 533).

3 Ticket Sales in German Professional Soccer

As already mentioned in chapter one, German clubs are selling a decent amount of their tickets. Especially the clubs in the First Bundesliga are able to sell out their tickets. However, many tickets are sold as season tickets in preseason:

Table 3: Available Seats and Season Tickets sold per Club First Bundesliga

Club	Available Seats	Season Tickets	Percentage
Borussia Dortmund	81360	55000	67.00%
Schalke 04	62271	43935	70.55%
Bayern München	75000	38000	50.67%
Borussia Mönchengladbach	54014	30000	55.54%
Eintracht Frankfurt	51500	27000	52.43%
Hamburger SV	57000	26000	45.61%
1. FC Köln	50000	25500	51.00%
Werder Bremen	42100	25000	59.38%
VFL Wolfsburg	30000	21500	71.67%
Hertha BSC	74649	20500	27.46%
RB Leipzig	42558	20000	47.00%
Bayer Leverkusen	30210	19000	62.89%
FSV Mainz	34000	19000	55.88%
FC Augsburg	30660	18500	60.34%
1899 Hoffenheim	30150	15000	49.75%
SC Freiburg	24000	15000	62.50%
FC Ingolstadt	15000	12000	80.00%
Darmstadt 98	17400	11500	66.09%
	801872	442435	57.54%

Source: Based on Statista.de 2017.

In 2016/2017 season, 442,435 out of 801,872 tickets are sold as season tickets. Also a few seasons earlier, "55% of all seats available in the Bundesliga were sold already weeks ahead of the 2011/2012 season kick-off" (Nufer, G.; Fischer, J., 2013: p. 53). This amount of season tickets seems to be steady throughout the last years. This means that less than half the tickets are sold to visitors on a game to game basis. In general, the top clubs and traditional (old) clubs are selling a larger percentage of their available tickets as season tickets. Borussia Dortmund, for example, is selling 55,000 out of 81,360 available tickets as season tickets. Another instance of this high rate of season tickets is Schalke 04, selling 43,935 out of 62,271 tickets as season tickets. Hertha BSC (Berlin) is selling marginal 27.46% of their tickets as season tickets. Overall, most of the teams of the First Bundesliga are selling more or around 50% of their available tickets as season tickets. Season tickets offer great discounts for the fans. In 2011/2012 season, "Borussia Dortmund offers about 30% discount on all seating categories and Bayern Munich tops the chart with 53% discount on tickets for its standing section" (Nufer, G.; Fischer, J., 2013: p. 53).

Only the remaining tickets are sold for the specific games during the season. There also has to be a contingent of tickets for fans of the visiting club. Moreover, one should recognize that only a fractional amount of the tickets are sold in the regular ticket sell in the First Bundesliga as it is presented in Table 3.

The clubs in the second German Bundesliga are selling a lower percentage of their tickets as season tickets:

Table 4: Available Seats and Season Tickets sold per Club Second Bundesliga

Club	Available Seats	Season Tickets	Percentage
VFB Stuttgart	60449	24500	40.53%
1. FC Nürnberg	50000	20000	40.00%
Hannover 96	49000	20000	40.82%
Dynamo Dresden	32066	17000	53.02%
Eintracht Braunschweig	23325	15000	64.31%
Fortuna Düsseldorf	54600	14600	26.74%
1. FC Kaiserslautern	49780	14000	28.12%
1. FC Union Berlin	22012	10000	45.43%
Arminia Bielefeld	26515	8000	30.17%
1. FC Heidenheim	15000	7400	49.33%
Karlsruher SC	28762	7000	24.34%
SpVgg Greuther Fürth	18000	4750	26.40%
Würzburger Kickers	13138	5900	44.91%
VFL Bochum	27599	5000	18.12%
FC Erzgebirge Aue	15690	3300	21.03%
SV Sandhausen	15414	2400	15.57%
FC St. Pauli	Not Relevant	Unknown	
TSV 1860 München	Not Relevant	Unknown	
	501350	178850	35.67%

Source: Based on Wikipedia.de 2017.

19

VFL Bochum, for example, is just selling 5,000 tickets out of 27,599 available seats as season tickets. Eintracht Braunschweig reaches the highest rate with 64.31%. This means that a higher percentage of tickets are for sale every game as it is presented in table 4. It is also important to make these fans with a season ticket come to the stadium as often as possible. Clubs must "understand their most avid fans and how to better satisfy them" to reach a "higher overall revenue from the additional dollars spent by on concessions and merchandise" (Castro Jr., S. M., 2014: p. 4). "Therefore knowing the factors which have the greatest impact on season ticket holders' attendance is important" (Castro Jr., S. M., 2014: p. 5). Furthermore, German clubs are binding these valuable fans to the club. Borussia Dortmund, for example, renewed 54,907 out 55,000 season tickets to the same holders after a mediocre season in 2014/2015 (Eurosport, 2015).

As stated in the introduction, the Second Bundesliga is not able to sell more than 64.61% of all tickets (season tickets included). Dynamic pricing "provides teams the flexibility to increase attendance for low demand games, by offering tickets at discounted prices" (Nufer, G.; Fischer, J., 2013: p. 56-57). Thus, current pricing strategies, as explained in the next chapter, fail selling remaining tickets on the market.

3.1   Pricing Strategies in German First and Second Bundesliga

The remaining tickets are sold with three different pricing strategies in the German professional soccer leagues:

1. Most of the clubs in the German leagues are setting fixed ticket prices at the beginning of the season. These prices will remain until the season is finished, and then the prices will be set again for the new season. All teams in the Second Bundesliga use this method for all regarded seasons.

2. Some clubs, especially in the first league, are charging a little more for top games. These matches are mostly announced before the season, and are derby's, or games against the top clubs like Bayern Munich or Borussia Dortmund. These games are more attractive for the fans concluding this sometimes small enhancement of the ticket prices. In season 2011/2012 for example, "the Hamburger SV and Hertha BSC Berlin

capitalize on strong ticket demand for their home games against Bayern Munich and Borussia Dortmund and charge up to 70% and 115% more compared to their games against the FC Augsburg and the SC Freiburg" (Nufer, G., Fischer, J., 2013: p. 52).

3. Only a few clubs use variable prices, and have different categories of prices depending on the game. These matches are categorized in the preseason most of the time. Categories are defined by above mentioned factors of attractiveness. RB Leipzig uses this method in 2016/2017 season. Eintracht Frankfurt uses this method only for their seating tickets in 2016/2017. In the years before this season, they used this method for all their tickets since 2012/2013. However, FC Köln was the first team to introduce categorized prices in the First Bundesliga. In season 2009/2010 Köln used this method until season 2012/2013, when they started in the Second Bundesliga. For this season, Köln switched to the first mentioned pricing strategy and stayed with it ever since. No club in the Second Bundesliga uses categorized prices for their tickets so far.

These three strategies have one significant disadvantage: Clubs cannot react to unforeseen events. Being on a winning streak, signing a new interesting player, a losing streak, or injuries cannot be taken into consideration for ticket prices. As mentioned before, clubs in the United States have introduced dynamic pricing models that help face these changes during a season. German clubs have not adapted dynamic pricing yet. The next section is going to analyze dynamic pricing in detail to show advantages and disadvantages concerning this more flexible pricing model.

3.2   Dynamic Pricing as the Future of Ticket Pricing in Sports

Opposing these outdated pricing strategies is Dynamic Pricing. If Dynamic Pricing is capable of taking numerous factors into account, then prices can be adapted in real-time depending on variables like weather, athletic situation or the day of the game. "The use of real-time information in sport ticket price setting runs counter to traditional marketing strategies where prices are fixed before the season (Shapiro, S.; Drayer, J.; 2012: p. 533). A few years ago, this would have been impossible due to the simple fact that a change in price would take far too much time. Nowadays, tickets are mostly purchased online so that a change in price can be completed in just a few seconds (Drayer, J.; Shapiro, S.; Lee, S., 2012: p. 187). Dynamic Pricing has already taken effect in a multiplicity of other sectors:

It started with Revenue Management during the 70's as it was introduced by the airline industry. "It resulted in significant revenue boosts for American Airlines and was quickly taken up by all other major airlines, such as Delta and United" (Nufer, G.; Fischer, J., 2013: p. 56). Only in a matter of time, Revenue Management became an attractive method in, for example, the airline industry, the hotel and holiday industry (cruise ships), and rental cars (Talluri K.; van Ryzen, G., 2004: p. 176).

In these areas it increases the general revenue and maximizes its use to capacity. Aside from these two benefits, by realizing dynamic pricing clubs are opening themselves to several risks a well:

1. There are more variables concerning the attractiveness of a sports game, than flights or hotel rooms. On one hand, aspects like weather or the team's position in the league are easy to quantify. But on the other hand, trades and signings to the team are more difficult to rate. Other factors that could determine the attractiveness of a match could be the time of the kickoff, holidays, size of the guest's fan club, and more. Dynamic Pricing works with an algorithm that is implicated to the web shop. Determining a working algorithm might be more difficult for the sports sector.

2. The fans will need to adjust to this change in the pricing strategy. They need to be educated so that they know why the strategy was changed, and how the new model works. Otherwise, fans might not understand the differences in price at different games. "Clubs should avoid giving fans the feeling that ticket prices are opportunistic" (Nufer, G.; Fischer, J., 2013: p. 55). This might lead to a general displeasure among the fans. Furthermore, by asking for higher prices to more interesting games, clubs end up pricing out some fans that would otherwise be able to afford a static ticket price. Guests might end up sitting next to each other on nearly the same spot, but having paid different prices because of the point in time they purchased their tickets. "If fans get used to dynamic pricing of football tickets, just like customers did in the case of airline tickets, dynamic pricing will also be the future of ticket pricing in European football" (Nufer, G.; Fischer, J., 2013: p. 58).

3. Problems might occur to holders of a season ticket. These fans are very valuable for the clubs because they pay money upfront for the whole season at the start. However, these

fans might pay too much money for unattractive games. If the team is playing bad during a given season, and the prices are therefore low the whole season, it could be that it would have been cheaper to buy individual tickets for each match. In conclusion, there is a risk of scaring fans off the season tickets.

4. As mentioned in point three, there is the opposing risk of ticket prices getting too expensive throughout the whole season. This makes tickets not affordable for certain groups of fans. Loosing young fans might be an especially dangerous prospect. A potential result might be that young people do not get in touch with soccer anymore. Therefore, leading to a loss of future generations' interest in the sport.

5. Changing a strategy can always lead to unforeseen problems. Especially for smaller clubs it might be a larger risk to change a working strategy.

These risks will be discussed again in the discussion of this thesis. However, as a reminder, "it can only be a matter of time before dynamic pricing will also find its way to the big arenas in European football" ((Nufer, G.; Fischer, J., 2013: p. 59).

3.3 Dynamic Pricing in German Soccer

During the last few years, there is a noticeable growth in the secondary ticket market. This indicates that German soccer clubs are missing out on potential ticket revenue, and these secondary distributors (for example: www.ticketbande.de) "are capitalizing on pricing inefficiencies in the primary market" (Drayer, J.; Shapiro, S.; Lee, S. 2012: p. 184). Even with current models, using fixed or variable pricing, "secondary market sellers have maintained their ability to respond to fluctuations in consumer demand in the days and even the hours leading up to an event" (Shapiro, S.; Drayer, J.; 2012: p. 532). Dynamic pricing strategies could offer a great solution to improve clubs revenues while still competing against the secondary ticket market. "Dynamic Pricing helps teams to compete with the secondary market by capturing some consumer surplus for high-demand games themselves" (Nufer, G.; Fischer, J., 2013: p. 56). "Closely aligning ticket prices with demand conditions will help teams to maximize their revenue from ticket sales and perhaps decrease the presence of sellers in the secondary market, who have long been associated with unethical practices" (Drayer, J.; Shapiro, S., 2009: p. 6).

In 1989, Kimes wrote an article about a dynamic pricing model, or revenue management system as it is also called, to improve revenue in the hotel industry. Based on this system for the hotel industry, published by Kimes in 1989, there are "six prerequisite circumstances for this pricing strategy to work" (Drayer, J.; Shapiro, S.; Lee, S., 2012: p. 3-4):

1. Market Segmentation: The managers of a hotel must be able to classify guests in different groups. This allows them to use different strategies among the different types of guests.

2. Perishable Inventory: In the hotel industry hotels cannot sell unused inventory (rooms) at a later point in time. An unused hotel room cannot be filled after the night is over.

3. Inventory sold in advance: Hotel rooms must be booked before the people are staying at the hotel. The closer a date gets, the more unlikely it will be that empty rooms will be booked. Therefore, it would be helpful to lower prices for closer dates (last-minute-sales).

4. Low marginal sales costs: Another guest staying in a hotel room does not cost much more money for the hotel. It would always be better to have someone staying in a hotel room for less money, than not having a guest in that room at all.

5. High marginal production costs: A hotel will not be able to easily add more rooms to its inventory. This means that prices in a hotel should be raised when it is close to being booked out. In the hotel industry this might be on holidays or when there are events nearby.

6. Changes in demand: Depending on different factors the demand of hotel rooms might change from time to time. Reasons, as previously mentioned, might be holidays, events, or the general season.

A few years later (1998) Kimes added a seventh criterion:

7. Predictability: The hotel must be able to analyze, and rate, the mentioned factors to adjust the prices for room. If hotels could not rate the demand of rooms, changes in price would be absurd (Drayer, J.; Shapiro, S.; Lee, S., 2012: p. 3-4).

"Based on these characteristics, it appears sporting event tickets are an appropriated environment for revenue management" (Shapiro, S.; Drayer, J.; 2012: p. 533). In the discussion, these criteria will be applied to German professional soccer leagues.

4 Discussion

Although these criteria were written for the hotel industry, they are also usable for other industries, such as the tourism sector in general. That being said, one should take a closer look at these criteria applied for the German soccer leagues:

1. German soccer clubs should be able to separate their guests in different categories. There are hardcore fans coming to every game, and staying in the fan-club segment of the stadium. There are guests coming on occasion like families and random spectators who may be sitting somewhere in the stadium. It might also be possible to segment fans by other criteria like income or age.

2. Seats or standing room that was not bought for a game cannot be sold afterwards. Therefore, clubs should always try to sell out for a game. Lowering prices for empty seats can help maximizing the ticket sales.

3. Most tickets are bought well in advance of the game, especially among the top teams in the league. Most people are not willing to take the risk to drive to the stadium, only to notice that the game is already sold out.

4. An additional fan visiting the game does not cost the club any more money. Furthermore, another fan coming to the stadium does bring the club more money. He might buy food, drinks, merchandise, and so on. An additional guest to a sporting event is even more valuable than another guest at a hotel. "With every additional supporter in the venue comes the opportunity for cross-selling" (Nufer, G.; Fischer, J., 2013: p. 57).

5. Like at a hotel, a club at the German soccer league will not be able to add additional seats or stands to the stadium. If a game is nearly sold out, clubs should raise prices for the remaining tickets.

6. Demands for tickets are affected by even more factors than booking at a hotel. Like mentioned before, there are many factors to be taken into consideration.

7. This might be the most difficult point to decide: Are these factors predictable? Because of the successful use of dynamic pricing in sports in the United States the answer to this question is yes. If dynamic pricing can help to improve the ticket revenue in the U.S., and help maximizing the number of visitors to the stadium, then German clubs should also be able to predict the request for tickets due to these factors.

Five risks of the introduction of dynamic pricing were mentioned in chapter 3.2. earlier. These risks can be regarded in consideration of this chapter again.

1. Point seven is the reason to answer the first mentioned risk: There are working algorithms, which allow teams in the United States to determine the attractiveness of sporting events. This, however, is just one of the five risks mentioned above.

2. The second risk is the education of the customer. Fans have to get used to this sort of pricing model. They have to understand that sitting next to each other does not mean that they have paid the same price for the ticket. Clubs should consider writing the highest possible price on every ticket so that these differences in prices are not seen by the fans directly. It might also increase the expected value of the ticket, and guests might feel better having paid less than it says on the ticket. People always like the feeling of making a great deal, and prefer that than the alternative. The alternative is to notice that they have paid more than the person sitting next to them. "As fans become more familiar with dynamic pricing, negative responses are likely to fade" (Nufer, G.; Fischer, J., 2013: p. 58).

3. The third possible problem mentioned is the situation of season ticket holders. A bad season and falling prices could potentially end in a bad deal for these valuable fans. As a solution, clubs should consider limits for the top prices as well as for the lower prices. This means that clubs should not act completely dynamic. They should ensure that holders of a season ticket still receive the best deal. If there are games for which prices for a ticket go below the price of a season ticket, then there should be added specials for season ticket holders for that game. Clubs might consider valuing the difference

for drinks or food to the holders of season tickets. It might also become more important to add specials in general for these most valuable fans. Meet and greet with the coach and the players, a jersey or a scarf coming with the ticket, free parking spots near the entrance, or a general discount for merchandise are just a few possibilities to think about.

4. The fourth risk mentioned also needs counteraction by the clubs. Pricing out valuable fans that might end up in losing future generations to the sport. In any case, there are practical solutions: The German leagues also show a tendency of keeping ticket prices low for some segments of the stadium, and at the same, charging more for top seats. This approach is also convertible to dynamic pricing. It would not be wise to introduce dynamic pricing to all tickets. The segment for the fan clubs should be priced steady. There should also be a segment for families with steady pricing throughout the season. However, dynamic pricing should be applied to the rest of the stadium on the long run due to the mentioned advantages.

5. The last risk or concern is that changing a strategy can always lead to problems. Especially smaller teams take a risk in changing a working strategy. Therefore, the change to dynamic pricing should not be started by smaller clubs playing in the second German league. It should be started by the international playing, top clubs in Germany, or by traditional clubs with a loyal fan base playing at the second German league.

However, especially the clubs in the Second Bundesliga should consider introducing dynamic pricing. This is due to mainly two introduced facts:

1. More tickets are sold every game compared to season tickets.

2. Stadium are not as highly filled on a regular basis compared to First Bundesliga

Dynamic pricing will help to sell more tickets in the Second Bundesliga, and higher the attractiveness of the experience of a visit to the stadium. Selling more tickets will also enhance the revenue of merchandise and accommodations inside the stadium.

With these arguments in mind, and these positive effects of the implementation of dynamic pricing in the United States, German clubs should be able to adapt this success. Thus, should attempt this pricing model. This conclusion is valuable for the First, as well as the second German league, with two different aims:

In the First Bundesliga, German clubs are able to sell most of their tickets to the stadium. This can be explained by many season ticket holders who are coming to the stadium regularly, and by low ticket prices compared to other top leagues in Europe. Maximizing the utilization of capacity is not an aim for these clubs. Dynamic pricing should be used to maximize the revenue of ticket sales. Third party distributors, who can sell tickets with a high profit margin, show that clubs in the first German league are missing on value there. Dynamic pricing will help cutting the revenue of third party distributors, and maximizing their own revenue.

In the Second Bundesliga, German clubs are not able to sell that many tickets to the stadium. Dynamic pricing will help to maximize the utilization of capacity. Therefore, help to enhance the general experience for the fans. This will also help to activate cross-selling and to maximize revenues from selling merchandise and other products at the stadium. It will also help to sell more season tickets for upcoming seasons because of a better atmosphere at the stadium. Second league clubs can catch up with the rates of season tickets of the first league. These fans are valuable for the clubs.

In concluding that dynamic pricing would help clubs maximizing both their ticket revenue and their use of capacity, there will be a time for another perspective of the situation: the perspective of the fans devoting themselves to a club. Critics say that these fans are afflicted negatively by the use of dynamic pricing, and by the clubs optimizing their business they are harming the average fan.

These concerns depend on the actual realization of dynamic pricing. If clubs focus on the fans while changing their strategies, fans can end in a fairer situation than before. Dynamic Pricing should try to take profit from third party distributors and not make more profit off the fans. Good deals for holders of season tickets, young and elder fans, and fan clubs might be essential for the acceptance of dynamic pricing among the guests.

The possibility of a crowded stadium every game might also improve the experience at the stadium. A breathtaking experience at the stadium might lead to one-time visitors becoming fans. It might thrill children or teenagers, and make them enthusiastic fans of soccer. This should be a general aim of the clubs: Generating young fans and make them play and love soccer. Many German clubs do a great job when it comes to youth work. This is essential for being successful in the future. Educating talented players is preferable over buying them from other countries. Getting more people in touch with the sport, in general, will also help to increase the number of children playing it. The more children playing it, the more talents can be discovered and educated. Maximizing the amount of visitors can have more consequences than just maximizing the profit of ticket sales.

German clubs should not try to raise the prices, because tickets are more expensive in other leagues. They should try to optimize their pricing strategy, because of the many positive effects that can occur for the clubs and for the fans.

The main risk of dynamic pricing that has to be discussed is that fans might be priced out of the stadium. This could lead to top games end up being played in front of "tourists", who want to experience a sporting event, instead of the real fans coming to the stadium every week. This risk can be minimized by other counteractions. In general, this risk is raised by third party distributors that will have less possibilities of selling tickets for absurd profit.

5 Further Research and Recommendations for Practitioners

For the realization and optimization of dynamic prices, more research must be done. Especially for the leading German clubs, which must try to switch to dynamic pricing. They should start a leading role in Europe. Therefore, they should do research on dynamic pricing at American sports. It needs to be analyzed how dynamic pricing is working overseas, and how it can be adapted to German leagues. This will help the lower leagues to adapt this pricing model, and help them to sell more tickets to their stadiums.

This Thesis, as most other empirical studies, has certain limitations. First limitation is that the considered time span is limited to ten years and that other influences, like inflation, is not taken into account. Also arguments, like the overall economic situation during this decade, are neglected. There are multiple factors that influence ticket sales at professional German soccer. Back in 2006 the World Cup took place in Germany. The sport was hyper influenced at a point where clubs could attract many fans the following years. The influence of this particular event is not analyzed as well.

This Thesis simplifies the representation of ticket prices within the First and the Second Bundesliga. Prices are categorized in four tiers, but there are many different prices in between these tiers. How many tickets there are sold, in which category, and how many different prices are existing in between these four tiers, is not taken into consideration. It is also not observed how much each club charges additional to the normal prices for top games. Surcharges are set different by every club, and can differ in the amount of money. Including the quantity during the season.

There should also be research among the acceptance of dynamic pricing in the United States. It would be helpful to analyze the mistakes that were made while switching to dynamic pricing. This research would help to avoid the same mistakes while implementing dynamic pricing in Germany.

German clubs should also consider working hand in hand with their own fans while introducing dynamic pricing. This would help to dodge misunderstandings and confusion in the beginning.

Research concerning the selling of season tickets will also be important. Further research should analyze these fans. How can clubs bind these fans? How can clubs make them come to all of their games?

Finally, an additional research topic would be how clubs can enhance fans' buying habits at the stadium.

References

Castro Jr., S. M. (2014). *Understanding Season Ticket Holders' Buying Behaviors.* Sport Management Undergraduate, Paper 7. Retrieved [06.07.2017], from fisherpub.sjfc.edu site: http://fisherpub.sjfc.edu/cgi/viewcontent.cgi?article=1004&context=sport_undergrad

Drayer, J.; Shapiro, S. (2009). *Value Determination in the Secondary Ticket Market: A Quantitative Analysis of the NFL Playoffs.* Sport Marketing Quarterly, 2009, 18, 5-13. Retrieved [04.07.2017], available at: http://papers.ssrn.com/sol3/papers.cfm?abstract_id=2457173

Drayer, J.; Shapiro, S.; Lee, S. (2012). *Dynamic Ticket Pricing in Sport: An Agenda for Research and Practice.* Sport Marketing Quarterly, 2012, 21, 184-194. Retrieved [28.06.2017], from Research Gate available at: https://www.researchgate.net/publication/264697964_Dynamic_Ticket_Pricing_in_Sport_An_Agenda_for_Research_and_Practice

Eurosport (2015). *55,000 season tickets on offer at Dortmund, only 93 weren't renewed for next season.* Retrieved [03.07.2017], from Eurosport available at: http://www.eurosport.com/football/55000-season-tickets-on-offer-at-dortmund-only-93-weren-t-renewed-for-next-season_sto4786723/story.shtml

Henderson, J. (2016). *Hello? Is everyone home? Soccer attendance in Italy is fading fast from fan protests, TV, economy.* Retrieved [03.07.2017], from johnhendersontravel.com site: http://johnhendersontravel.com/2016/12/15/hello-is-everyone-home-soccer-attendance-in-italy-is-fading-fast-from-fan-protests-tv-economy/

Kaplan, D. (2015). *Dynamic ticket pricing makes successful debut in NFL.* Retrieved [03.07.2017], from Sportsbusinessdaily: http://www.sportsbusinessdaily.com/Journal/Issues/2015/10/26/Leagues-and-Governing-Bodies/NFL-dynamic.aspx

Kelly, D. (2016). *Why are Serie A attendances so low this season?* Retrieved [03.07.2017], from Newstalk.com site:

http://www.newstalk.com/podcasts/Off_The_Ball/The_Football_Show_on_Off_The_Ball/121 508/Klopp_in_control_Neville_in_trouble_Serie_A_decline

Kimes, S.E. (1989). *The basic of yield management [Electronic version].* Cornell Hotel and Restaurant Administration Quarterly, 30(3), 14-19. Retrieved [30.06.2017], from Cornell University, School of Hospitality Administration site:

http://scholarship.sha.cornell.edu/articles/456/

Kimes, S.E., Chase, R.B., Choi, S., Lee, P.Y. & Ngonzi, E.N. (1998). *Restaurant revenue management: Applying yield management to the restaurant industry [Electronic version].* Cornell Hotel and Restaurant Administration Quarterly, 39(3), 32-39. Retrieved [01.07.2017], from Cornell University, School of Hospitality Administration site:

http://scholarship.sha.cornell.edu/articles/460/

Michaels, C. (2017). *Top 16 Most Expensive Sports Tickets.* Retrieved [03.07.2017], from barrystickets.com site:

https://www.barrystickets.com/blog/15-most-expensive-sports-tickets/

Nufer, G.; Fischer, J. (2013). *Ticket Pricing in European Football – Analysis and Implications.* Sport and Art 1(2): 49-60, 2013. Retrieved [05.07.2017], from hrpub.org available at:

http://www.hrpub.org/download/201309/saj.2013.010205.pdf

Rishe, P. (2012). *Dynamic Pricing: The Future of Ticket Pricing in Sports [Electronic version].* Retrieved [03.07.2017], from Forbes.com site:

http://www.forbes.com/sites/prishe/2012/01/06/dynamic-pricing-the-future-of-ticket-pricing-in-sports/#64dc29fe600f

Shapiro, S.; Drayer, J. (2012). *A New Age of Demand-Based Pricing: An Examination of Dynamic Ticket Pricing and Secondary Market Prices in Major League Baseball.* Journal of Sport Management, 2012, 26, 532-546. Retrieved [09.07.2017], available at: https://www.researchgate.net/publication/264697628_A_New_Age_of_Demand-Based_Pricing_An_Examination_of_Dynamic_Ticket_Pricing_and_Secondary_Market_Prices_in_Major_League_Baseball

Soccerstats (2017). *England – Premier League Home attendances.* Retrieved [03.07.2017], from Soccerstats available at: http://www.soccerstats.com/attendance.asp?league=england

Statista (2017). *Umsatz der Vereine in der 1. Fußball-Bundesliga in der Saison 2015/2016 (in Millionen Euro).* Retrieved [03.07.2017], from Statista available at: https://de.statista.com/statistik/daten/studie/192749/umfrage/umsatz-deutscher-bundesligavereine/

Statista (2017a). *Average ticket prices in the major sports leagues in North America 2015/16* Retrieved [03.07.2017], from Statista available at: https://www.statista.com/statistics/261588/average-ticket-price-major-us-sports-leagues/

Talluri K.T.; van Ryzen G.J. (2004). *The Theory and Practice of Revenue Management.* Springer.

Transfermarkt (2017). *First Bundesliga Besucherzahlen 16/17.* Retrieved [03.07.2017], from Transfermarkt available at: https://www.transfermarkt.de/1-bundesliga/besucherzahlen/wettbewerb/L1/plus/?saison_id=2016

Transfermarkt (2017a). *Second Bundesliga Besucherzahlen 16/17.* Retrieved [03.07.2017], from Transfermarkt available at: https://www.transfermarkt.de/1-bundesliga/besucherzahlen/wettbewerb/L2/plus/?saison_id=2016

Unknown. (2013). *How do ticket prices for the Premier League compare with Europe?* Retrieved [01.07.2017], from The Guardian available at: https://theguardian.com/news/datablog/2013/jan/17/football-ticket-prices-premier-league-europe

Willens, M. (2015). *MLS Tickets more expensive than Bundesliga, Ligue 1, and most other top European leagues.* Retrieved [11.07.2017], from International Business Time site: http://www.ibtimes.com/mls-tickets-more-expensive-bundesliga-ligue-1-most-other-top-european-leagues-2110361

Wikipedia, (2017). *Fußball-Bundesliga 2016/17.* Retrieved [01.07.2017], from Wikipedia available at: https://de.wikipedia.org/wiki/Fu%C3%9Fball-Bundesliga_2016/17

Wikipedia, (2017a). *2. Fußball-Bundesliga 2016/17.* Retrieved [01.07.2017], from Wikipedia available at: https://de.wikipedia.org/wiki/2._Fu%C3%9Fball-Bundesliga_2016/17

Appendix

Visitors at German first and Second Bundesliga over the last ten years:

Sport Bild Sonderheft Bundesliga Saison 2007/2008

Sport Bild Sonderheft Bundesliga Saison 2008/2009

Sport Bild Sonderheft Bundesliga Saison 2009/2010

Sport Bild Sonderheft Bundesliga Saison 2010/2011

Sport Bild Sonderheft Bundesliga Saison 2011/2012

Sport Bild Sonderheft Bundesliga Saison 2012/2013

Sport Bild Sonderheft Bundesliga Saison 2013/2014

Sport Bild Sonderheft Bundesliga Saison 2014/2015

Sport Bild Sonderheft Bundesliga Saison 2015/2016

Sport Bild Sonderheft Bundesliga Saison 2016/2017

Visitors 2016/2017 for European Leagues available at:

https://www.transfermarkt.de/1-bundesliga/besucherzahlen/wettbewerb/L1

https://www.transfermarkt.de/2-bundesliga/besucherzahlen/wettbewerb/L2

https://www.transfermarkt.de/premier-league/besucherzahlen/wettbewerb/GB1

https://www.transfermarkt.de/serie-a/besucherzahlen/wettbewerb/IT1

https://www.transfermarkt.de/ligue-1/besucherzahlen/wettbewerb/FR1

Season Ticket sales available at:

First Bundesliga:

https://de.statista.com/statistik/daten/studie/163863/umfrage/dauerkarten-fuer-die-
  bundesligasaison-nach-vereinen/

Second Bundesliga:

https://de.wikipedia.org/wiki/2._Fu%C3%9Fball-Bundesliga_2016/17

Tables of ticket prices in the First Bundesliga:

Season 2007/08:

Team	Standing Room		Seats	
	Low	High	Low	High
VFB Stuttgart	9,00€	18,00€	17,00€	70,90€
FC Schalke 04	8,00€	11,00€	17,00€	52,00€
Werder Bremen	10,00€	13,00€	12,00€	50,00€
FC Bayern Munich	12,00€	12,00€	20,00€	50,00€
Bayer Leverkusen			13,50€	37,00€
FC Nürnberg	10,00€		13,00€	55,00€
Hamburger SV	9,00€	16,00€	15,00€	70,00€
VFL Bochum	8,00€	11,00€	10,00€	35,00€
Borussia Dortmund	8,00€	12,00€	23,50€	55,00€
Hertha BSC Berlin			9,00€	69,00€
Arminia Bielefeld	10,00€	12,00€	19,00€	50,00€
Energie Cottbus	10,00€	13,00€	16,00€	34,00€
Eintracht Frankfurt	11,00€	14,00€	18,00€	55,00€
VFL Wolfsburg	9,00€	12,00€	17,00€	42,00€
Karlsruher SC	7,00€	12,00€	15,00€	40,00€
Hansa Rostock	8,00€	12,00€	17,00€	39,00€
MSV Duisburg	5,00€	10,00€	11,50€	40,00€
Hannover 96		Unknown		
Average	8,93€	12,71€	15,50€	49,64€

Season 2008/09:

Team	Standing Room		Seats	
	Low	High	Low	High
VFB Stuttgart	12,00€	19,10€	19,00€	67,50€
FC Schalke 04	10,00€	13,00€	19,00€	53,00€
Werder Bremen	8,00€	16,00€	17,00€	55,00€
FC Bayern Munich	12,00€	15,00€	20,00€	60,00€
Bayer Leverkusen			20,50€	37,00€
Hamburger SV	12,00€	19,00€	12,00€	84,00€
VFL Bochum	8,00€	13,00€	10,00€	40,00€
Borussia Dortmund	7,60€	12,50€	29,00€	57,00€
Hertha BSC Berlin			10,50€	71,50€
Arminia Bielefeld	10,00€	10,00€	19,00€	49,00€
Energie Cottbus	8,50€	12,00€	15,00€	28,00€
Eintracht Frankfurt	12,00€	14,00€	19,00€	56,00€
VFL Wolfsburg	6,00€	11,00€	6,00€	40,00€
Karlsruher SC	10,00€	12,00€	15,00€	40,00€
Hannover 96	6,00€	13,00€	16,00€	48,00€
Borussia Mönchengladbach	8,50€	12,00€	20,00€	39,50€
FC Köln	8,00€	11,00€	18,00€	51,00€
TSG Hoffenheim	11,00€	11,00€	21,00€	36,00€
Average	9,35€	13,35€	17,00€	50,69€

Season 2009/10:

Team	Standing Room		Seats	
	Low	High	Low	High
VFB Stuttgart	7,00€	20,00€	12,00€	75,00€
FC Schalke 04	10,00€	13,00€	19,00€	53,00€
Werder Bremen	8,00€	16,00€	17,00€	55,00€
FC Bayern Munich	12,00€	15,00€	20,00€	70,00€
Bayer Leverkusen	10,00€	13,50€	20,00€	42,00€
FC Nürnberg	9,00€	13,00€	11,00€	47,00€
Hamburger SV	9,00€	19,00€	15,00€	84,00€
VFL Bochum	11,00€	15,00€	25,00€	45,00€
Borussia Dortmund	8,50€	14,00€	26,50€	63,00€
Hertha BSC Berlin			11,00€	76,00€
Eintracht Frankfurt	12,00€	14,00€	19,00€	56,00€
VFL Wolfsburg	6,00€	12,00€	11,00€	46,00€
Hannover 96	6,00€	13,00€	10,00€	48,00€
Mainz 05	12,50€	12,50€	18,00€	37,00€
Borussia Mönchengladbach	9,50€	13,00€	21,00€	40,50€
SC Freiburg	10,00€	12,00€	30,00€	42,00€
FC Köln	Seats are variable depending on the categorie of the opponent			
TSG Hoffenheim	12,00€	12,00€	26,00€	41,00€
Average	9,53€	14,19€	18,32€	54,15€

Season 2010/11:

Team	Standing Room		Seats	
	Low	High	Low	High
VFB Stuttgart	7,00€	18,00€	12,00€	80,00€
FC Schalke 04	15,00€	15,00€	30,00€	50,00€
Werder Bremen	11,00€	16,00€	20,00€	55,00€
FC Bayern Munich	12,00€	15,00€	25,00€	70,00€
Bayer Leverkusen	10,00€	13,50€	20,00€	42,00€
FC Nürnberg	9,00€	13,00€	11,00€	47,00€
Hamburger SV	12,00€	19,00€	15,00€	84,00€
Borussia Dortmund	9,00€	14,50€	27,50€	65,00€
Eintracht Frankfurt	12,00€	15,00€	20,00€	62,00€
VFL Wolfsburg	6,00€	12,00€	11,00€	44,00€
Hannover 96	6,00€	13,00€	10,00€	48,00€
Mainz 05	18,00€	37,00€	12,50€	
Borussia Mönchengladbach	9,50€	13,00€	21,00€	40,50€
SC Freiburg	10,00€	12,00€	30,00€	42,00€
FC Kaiserslautern	9,50€	13,00€	15,00€	47,00€
FC Köln	Seats are variable depending on the categorie of the opponent			
FC St. Pauli		Unknown		
TSG Hoffenheim	12,00€	12,00€	26,00€	41,00€
Average	10,50€	15,69€	19,13€	54,50€

Season 2011/12:

Team	Standing Room		Seats	
	Low	High	Low	High
VFB Stuttgart	7,00€	13,00€	13,00€	52,00€
FC Schalke 04	15,00€	15,00€	30,00€	50,00€
Werder Bremen	11,00€	16,00€	20,00€	55,00€
FC Bayern Munich	15,00€	15,00€	30,00€	70,00€
Bayer Leverkusen	10,00€	13,50€	20,00€	42,00€
FC Nürnberg	9,00€	13,00€	11,00€	47,00€
Hamburger SV	12,00€	19,00€	15,00€	84,00€
Borussia Dortmund	10,30€	14,90€	28,20€	67,00€
Hertha BSC Berlin			10,00€	68,00€
VFL Wolfsburg		Unknown		
Hannover 96	6,00€	13,00€	10,00€	48,00€
Mainz 05	12,50€	12,50€	18,00€	42,00€
Borussia Mönchenglad-bach	9,50€	13,00€	21,00€	40,50€
SC Freiburg	10,00€	12,00€	30,00€	42,00€
FC Kaiserslautern	11,00€	14,00€	19,00€	44,00€
FC Augsburg	11,00€	13,00€	19,00€	39,00€
FC Köln	Seats are variable depending on the categorie of the opponent			
TSG Hoffenheim	12,00€	12,00€	26,00€	41,00€
Average	10,75€	13,93€	20,01€	51,97€

Season 2012/13:

Team	Standing Room		Seats	
	Low	High	Low	High
VFB Stuttgart	8,00€	18,00€	14,00€	72,00€
FC Schalke 04	15,50€	15,50€	26,00€	52,00€
Werder Bremen	11,00€	16,00€	20,00€	55,00€
FC Bayern Munich	15,00€	15,00€	30,00€	70,00€
Bayer Leverkusen	5,00€	15,00€	12,00€	76,00€
FC Nürnberg	13,00€	15,00€	23,00€	52,00€
Hamburger SV	10,00€	19,00€	20,00€	94,00€
Borussia Dortmund	10,30€	15,30€	29,00€	50,00€
Eintracht Frankfurt	Seats are variable depending on the categorie of the opponent			
VFL Wolfsburg	6,00€	12,00€	11,00€	44,00€
Hannover 96	6,00€	14,00€	10,00€	52,00€
Mainz 05	12,50€	12,50€	18,00€	60,00€
SC Freiburg	10,00€	12,00€	30,00€	42,00€
Greuther Fürth	13,00€	19,00€	16,00€	41,00€
FC Augsburg	11,00€	13,00€	23,00€	39,00€
TSG Hoffenheim	12,00€	12,00€	20,00€	41,00€
Fortuna Düsseldorf	13,00€	17,00€	17,00€	46,00€
TSG Hoffenheim		Unknown		
Average	10,71€	15,02€	19,94€	55,38€

Season 2013/14:

Team	Standing Room		Seats	
	Low	High	Low	High
VFB Stuttgart	8,00€	18,00€	14,00€	72,00€
FC Schalke 04	15,50€	15,50€	26,00€	52,00€
Werder Bremen	11,00€	16,00€	20,00€	65,00€
FC Bayern Munich	15,00€	15,00€	30,00€	70,00€
Bayer Leverkusen	6,00€	18,00€	12,00€	76,00€
FC Nürnberg	14,00€	16,00€	24,00€	54,00€
Hamburger SV	10,00€	16,00€	20,00€	94,00€
Borussia Dortmund	10,30€	15,30€	29,00€	50,00€
Hertha BSC Berlin			15,00€	89,00€
Eintracht Frankfurt	Seats are variable depending on the categorie of the opponent			
VFL Wolfsburg	6,00€	15,00€	11,00€	44,00€
Hannover 96	6,00€	14,00€	10,00€	52,00€
Mainz 05	12,50€	12,50€	18,00€	60,00€
Borussia Mönchenglad-bach	11,00€	14,50€	24,00€	30,50€
SC Freiburg	11,00€	14,00€	32,00€	46,00€
FC Augsburg	11,00€	13,00€	23,00€	39,00€
TSG Hoffenheim	12,00€	12,00€	20,00€	41,00€
Eintracht Braunschweig	11,00€	16,00€	6,00€	33,00€
Average	10,64€	15,05€	19,65€	56,91€

Season 2014/15:

Team	Standing Room		Seats	
	Low	High	Low	High
VFB Stuttgart	8,50€	19,50€	15,00€	87,50€
FC Schalke 04	15,50€	15,50€	26,00€	52,00€
Werder Bremen	12,00€	16,00€	20,00€	70,00€
FC Bayern Munich	15,00€	15,00€	30,00€	70,00€
Bayer Leverkusen	10,00€	15,00€	10,00€	68,00€
Hamburger SV	14,00€	16,00€	20,00€	94,00€
Borussia Dortmund	10,70€	16,40€	30,70€	53,50€
Hertha BSC Berlin			15,00€	96,00€
Eintracht Frankfurt	Seats are variable depending on the categorie of the opponent			
VFL Wolfsburg	5,00€	15,00€	15,00€	70,00€
Hannover 96	6,00€	14,00€	10,00€	52,00€
Mainz 05	12,50€	12,50€	18,00€	60,00€
Borussia Mönchenglad-bach	11,00€	14,50€	24,00€	44,50€
SC Freiburg	11,00€	14,50€	33,00€	62,00€
FC Augsburg	14,00€	14,00€	25,00€	39,00€
FC Köln	9,50€	16,00€	23,00€	65,00€
SC Paderborn 07	12,00€	16,00€	25,00€	60,00€
TSG Hoffenheim	12,00€	17,00€	20,00€	70,00€
Average	11,17€	15,43€	21,16€	65,50€

Season 2015/16:

Team	Standing Room		Seats	
	Low	High	Low	High
VFB Stuttgart	8,50€	19,50€	15,00€	87,50€
FC Schalke 04	15,50€	15,50€	26,00€	52,00€
Werder Bremen	12,00€	16,00€	20,00€	70,00€
FC Bayern Munich	15,00€	15,00€	35,00€	70,00€
Bayer Leverkusen	10,00€	15,00€	10,00€	68,00€
Hamburger SV	14,00€	16,00€	20,00€	94,00€
Borussia Dortmund	10,90€	16,20€	21,90€	54,40€
Hertha BSC Berlin			15,00€	96,00€
Eintracht Frankfurt	Seats are variable depending on the categorie of the opponent			
VFL Wolfsburg	5,00€	15,00€	15,00€	70,00€
Hannover 96	6,00€	14,00€	10,00€	54,00€
Mainz 05	12,50€	12,50€	18,00€	60,00€
Borussia Mönchenglad-bach	11,00€	14,50€	24,00€	44,50€
FC Augsburg	14,00€	14,00€	25,00€	45,00€
FC Köln	9,50€	16,00€	16,00€	65,00€
TSG Hoffenheim	12,00€	17,00€	20,00€	80,00€
FC Ingolstadt	14,00€	14,00€	17,00€	45,00€
SV Darmstadt	15,00€	18,00€	24,00€	40,00€
Average	11,56€	15,51€	19,52€	64,44€

Season 2016/17:

Team	Standing Room		Seats	
	Low	High	Low	High
FC Schalke 04	15,50€	15,50€	26,00€	52,00€
Werder Bremen	15,00€	15,00€	15,00€	70,00€
FC Bayern Munich	15,00€	15,00€	35,00€	70,00€
Bayer Leverkusen	10,00€	15,00€	10,00€	68,00€
Hamburger SV	15,00€	17,00€	21,00€	95,00€
Borussia Dortmund	10,90€	16,70€	21,90€	54,40€
Hertha BSC Berlin			15,00€	99,00€
Eintracht Frankfurt	15,00€	15,00€	Seats are variable depending on the opponent	
VFL Wolfsburg	5,00€	15,00€	15,00€	70,00€
Mainz 05	12,50€	12,50€	18,00€	60,00€
Borussia Mönchenglad-bach	11,00€	17,00€	19,90€	64,50€
SC Freiburg	13,00€	19,00€	34,00€	72,00€
FC Augsburg	14,00€	14,00€	25,00€	45,00€
FC Köln	9,50€	16,00€	16,00€	75,00€
TSG Hoffenheim	12,00€	18,00€	20,00€	70,00€
FC Ingolstadt	14,00€	14,00€	17,00€	44,00€
RB Leipzig	Seats are variable depending on the categorie of the opponent			
SV Darmstadt	15,00€	18,00€	24,00€	40,00€
Average	12,65€	15,79€	20,80€	65,56€

Tables of ticket prices in the Second Bundesliga:

Season 2007/08:

Team	Standing Room		Seats	
	Low	High	Low	High
Mainz 05	10,00€	10,00€	13,00€	32,00€
Alemannia Aachen	5,00€	13,00€	20,50€	28,50€
Borussia Mönchengladbach	7,00€	10,00€	16,00€	31,50€
SC Freiburg	4,00€	8,50€	6,00€	35,00€
Greuther Fürth	9,50€	9,50€	13,00€	20,50€
FC Kaiserslautern	9,00€	9,00€	13,50€	35,00€
FC Augsburg	9,00€	9,00€	14,00€	28,00€
TSV 1860 Munich	10,50€	10,50€	21,00€	31,50€
FC Köln	5,00€	9,00€	15,00€	46,00€
FC Erzgebirge Aue	8,00€	8,00€	11,00€	22,00€
SC Paderborn 07	3,50€	9,50€	5,00€	21,00€
TuS Koblenz	10,00€	10,00€	15,00€	25,00€
FC Carlzeiss Jena	7,00€	9,00€	8,00€	21,00€
Offenbacher FC	4,00€	10,00€	12,00€	29,00€
FC St. Pauli	8,00€	13,00€	13,00€	150,00€
SV Wiesbaden	10,00€	10,00€	20,50€	28,50€
TSG Hoffenheim	4,00€	9,00€	17,50€	23,50€
VFL Osnabrück	4,00€	10,00€	20,00€	25,00€
Average	7,08€	9,82€	14,11€	35,17€

Season 2008/09:

Team	Standing Room		Seats	
	Low	High	Low	High
FC Nürnberg	9,00€	13,00€	11,00€	47,00€
Hansa Rostock	7,00€	11,00€	14,00€	23,00€
MSV Duisburg	6,00€	9,00€	10,00€	110,00€
Mainz 05	10,50€	10,50€	14,00€	33,00€
Alemannia Aachen	5,00€	13,00€	20,50€	28,50€
SC Freiburg	8,00€	8,50€	20,00€	35,00€
Greuther Fürth	10,00€	10,00€	7,00€	20,50€
FC Kaiserslautern	9,00€	9,00€	15,50€	35,00€
FC Augsburg	9,00€	9,00€	7,00€	28,00€
TSV 1860 Munich	10,50€	10,50€	21,00€	31,50€
TuS Koblenz	11,50€	11,50€	17,00€	27,00€
FC St. Pauli	11,00€	13,00€	22,00€	45,00€
VFL Osnabrück	5,00€	12,00€	24,00€	35,00€
RW Oberhausen	6,50€	8,00€	8,50€	23,00€
FSV Frankfurt	7,00€	9,00€	15,00€	35,00€
FC Ingolstadt	8,00€	13,00€	20,00€	40,00€
RW Ahlen	6,00€	9,00€	13,00€	23,00€
SV Wehen		Unknown		
Average	8,18€	10,38€	15,26€	36,44€

Season 2009/10:

Team	Standing Room		Seats	
	Low	High	Low	High
Arminia Bielefeld	10,00€	10,00€	17,00€	36,00€
Energie Cottbus	8,50€	10,50€	13,00€	25,00€
Karlsruher SC	6,00€	11,00€	13,00€	35,00€
Hansa Rostock	7,00€	11,00€	14,00€	32,00€
MSV Duisburg	4,50€	9,00€	4,50€	110,00€
Alemannia Aachen	6,50€	12,50€	7,50€	40,00€
Greuther Fürth	10,00€	10,00€	8,50€	24,00€
FC Kaiserslautern	11,00€	11,00€	17,50€	36,50€
FC Augsburg	10,00€	12,00€	18,00€	33,00€
TSV 1860 Munich	8,00€	14,00€	15,00€	38,00€
SC Paderborn 07	11,50€	11,50€	18,00€	25,00€
TuS Koblenz	5,50€	11,50€	17,00€	35,00€
FC St. Pauli	11,00€	13,00€	22,00€	45,00€
RW Oberhausen	7,00€	10,00€	9,00€	32,00€
FSV Frankfurt	5,00€	9,00€	15,00€	30,00€
RW Ahlen	10,00€	11,00€	22,00€	30,00€
FC Union Berlin	9,00€	10,00€	19,00€	25,00€
Fortuna Düsseldorf			11,00€	35,00€
Average	8,26€	11,06€	14,50€	37,03€

Season 2010/11:

Team	Standing Room		Seats	
	Low	High	Low	High
VFL Bochum	8,00€	11,00€	25,00€	35,00€
Hertha BSC Berlin			9,50€	47,50€
Arminia Bielefeld	9,00€	11,00€	20,00€	30,00€
Energie Cottbus	8,50€	10,50€	13,00€	24,00€
Karlsruher SC	6,00€	11,00€	13,00€	35,00€
MSV Duisburg	4,50€	9,00€	4,50€	110,00€
Alemannia Aachen	6,50€	12,50€	7,50€	40,00€
Greuther Fürth	10,00€	10,00€	8,50€	24,00€
FC Augsburg	10,00€	12,00€	16,00€	33,00€
TSV 1860 Munich	8,00€	14,00€	15,00€	38,00€
FC Erzgebirge Aue	10,00€	10,00€	10,00€	22,00€
SC Paderborn 07	12,00€	12,00€	22,00€	30,00€
VFL Osnabrück	5,00€	12,00€	7,50€	32,00€
RW Oberhausen	7,00€	10,00€	9,00€	32,00€
FSV Frankfurt	5,00€	9,00€	10,00€	30,00€
FC Ingolstadt	5,00€	11,00€	9,00€	26,00€
FC Union Berlin	8,00€	11,00€	14,00€	26,00€
Fortuna Düsseldorf	6,00€			38,00€
Average	7,56€	11,00€	12,56€	36,25€

Season 2011/12:

Team	Standing Room		Seats	
	Low	High	Low	High
Energie Cottbus	8,50€	10,50€	13,00€	24,00€
Eintracht Frankfurt	10,00€	10,00€		45,00€
Karlsruher SC	6,00€	11,00€	13,00€	35,00€
Hansa Rostock	7,00€	10,00€	11,00€	34,00€
MSV Duisburg	5,00€	10,00€	4,50€	33,00€
Alemannia Aachen	6,50€	12,50€	7,50€	40,00€
Greuther Fürth	10,00€	10,00€	8,50€	24,00€
TSV 1860 Munich	7,00€	14,00€	9,95€	36,00€
SC Paderborn 07	12,00€	12,00€	22,00€	30,00€
FC St. Pauli	8,00€	13,00€	20,00€	40,00€
FSV Frankfurt	5,00€	9,00€	10,00€	30,00€
FC Ingolstadt	5,00€	11,00€	9,00€	26,00€
FC Union Berlin	10,00€	11,00€	16,00€	26,00€
Fortuna Düsseldorf	6,00€			38,00€
Eintracht Braun-schweig	8,00€	11,00€	16,00€	26,00€
Dynamo Dresden	7,50€	11,50€	11,50€	30,00€
Average	7,59€	11,14€	12,28€	32,31€

Season 2012/13:

Team	Standing Room		Seats	
	Low	High	Low	High
VFL Bochum	8,00€	12,00€	20,00€	35,00€
Hertha BSC Berlin			10,00€	48,00€
Energie Cottbus	8,50€	10,50€	13,00€	24,00€
MSV Duisburg	5,00€	10,00€	4,50€	33,00€
FC Kaiserslautern	11,00€	11,00€	15,50€	38,50€
TSV 1860 Munich	7,00€	14,00€	9,95€	36,00€
FC Köln	9,00€	13,00€	12,00€	49,00€
FC Erzgebirge Aue	10,00€	10,00€	10,00€	22,00€
SC Paderborn 07	12,00€	12,00€	22,00€	30,00€
FC St. Pauli	9,00€	14,00€	22,00€	42,00€
FSV Frankfurt	5,00€	9,00€	10,00€	30,00€
FC Ingolstadt	4,50€	10,00€	10,00€	23,50€
FC Union Berlin	10,00€	11,00€	16,00€	26,00€
Eintracht Braun-schweig	8,00€	11,00€	16,00€	26,00€
Dynamo Dresden	7,50€	11,50€	11,50€	33,00€
SV Sandhausen	7,00€	13,00€	11,00€	21,00€
VFR Aalen	4,00€	11,00€	6,00€	30,00€
SSV Jahn	6,00€	12,00€	15,00€	25,00€
Average	7,74€	11,44€	13,03€	31,78€

Season 2013/14:

Team	Standing Room		Seats	
	Low	High	Low	High
VFL Bochum	8,00€	12,00€	20,00€	35,00€
Arminia Bielefeld	9,00€	13,00€	12,00€	26,00€
Energie Cottbus	8,50€	10,50€	13,00€	24,00€
Karlsruher SC	11,00€	12,00€	15,00€	39,00€
Greuther Fürth	10,00€	10,00€	8,50€	24,00€
FC Kaiserslautern	11,00€	11,00€	15,50€	38,50€
TSV 1860 Munich	7,00€	14,00€	9,95€	36,00€
FC Köln	9,00€	13,00€	12,00€	49,00€
FC Erzgebirge Aue	10,00€	10,00€	10,00€	22,00€
SC Paderborn 07	12,00€	12,00€	22,00€	30,00€
FC St. Pauli	9,00€	14,00€	22,00€	42,00€
FSV Frankfurt	5,00€	10,00€	10,00€	30,00€
FC Ingolstadt	4,50€	10,00€	10,00€	23,50€
FC Union Berlin	8,00€	11,00€	26,00€	40,00€
Fortuna Düsseldorf	6,00€			38,00€
Dynamo Dresden	8,00€	12,50€	10,00€	34,00€
SV Sandhausen	7,00€	13,00€	11,00€	21,00€
VFR Aalen	5,00€	14,00€	7,00€	33,00€
Average	8,22€	11,88€	13,76€	32,50€

Season 2014/15:

Team	Standing Room		Seats	
	Low	High	Low	High
FC Nürnberg	13,00€	13,00€	22,00€	46,00€
VFL Bochum	9,00€	13,00€	27,00€	37,00€
Karlsruher SC	11,00€	12,00€	15,00€	39,00€
Greuther Fürth	12,00€	12,00€	15,00€	32,00€
FC Kaiserslautern	11,00€	11,00€	15,50€	38,50€
TSV 1860 Munich	7,00€	14,00€	9,95€	36,00€
FC Erzgebirge Aue	10,00€	10,00€	10,00€	22,00€
FC St. Pauli	9,00€	14,00€	22,00€	42,00€
FSV Frankfurt	5,00€	10,00€	10,00€	33,00€
FC Ingolstadt	4,50€	10,00€	10,00€	23,50€
FC Union Berlin	11,00€	13,00€	28,00€	40,00€
Fortuna Düsseldorf	6,00€			38,00€
Eintracht Braun-schweig	10,00€	14,00€	6,00€	31,00€
SV Sandhausen	7,00€	13,00€	10,00€	28,00€
VFR Aalen	7,00€	14,00€	9,00€	28,00€
FC Heidenheim	2,00€	13,00€	5,50€	200,00€
RB Leipzig			10,00€	30,00€
SV Darmstadt	12,00€	12,00€	20,00€	30,00€
Average	8,62€	12,33€	14,41€	43,00€

Season 2015/16:

Team	Standing Room		Seats	
	Low	High	Low	High
FC Nürnberg	13,00€	13,00€	20,00€	46,00€
VFL Bochum	9,00€	12,00€	15,00€	37,00€
Arminia Bielefeld	10,00€	12,00€	13,00€	26,00€
Karlsruher SC	11,00€	12,00€	15,00€	39,00€
MSV Duisburg	6,00€	12,00€	4,50€	34,00€
SC Freiburg	10,50€	12,00€	27,00€	52,00€
Greuther Fürth	12,00€	12,00€	15,00€	32,00€
FC Kaiserslautern	12,00€	12,00€	16,50€	41,00€
TSV 1860 Munich	7,00€	14,00€	9,95€	36,00€
SC Paderborn 07	12,00€	14,00€	24,00€	35,00€
FC St. Pauli	9,00€	14,50€	22,50€	43,00€
FSV Frankfurt	5,00€	10,00€	12,00€	35,00€
FC Union Berlin	11,00€	13,00€	28,00€	40,00€
Fortuna Düsseldorf	6,00€			38,00€
Eintracht Braun-schweig	10,00€	14,00€	6,00€	31,00€
SV Sandhausen	11,00€	13,00€	20,00€	28,00€
FC Heidenheim	2,50€	13,00€	6,50€	31,00€
RB Leipzig			10,00€	30,00€
Average	9,24€	12,63€	15,59€	36,33€

Season 2016/17:

Team	Standing Room		Seats	
	Low	High	Low	High
VFB Stuttgart	14,50€	14,50€		55,50€
FC Nürnberg	13,00€	13,00€	20,00€	46,00€
VFL Bochum	9,00€	12,00€	15,00€	37,00€
Arminia Bielefeld	10,00€	12,00€	13,00€	26,00€
Karlsruher SC	11,00€	12,00€	15,00€	39,00€
Hannover 96	12,00€	12,00€	20,00€	38,00€
Greuther Fürth	12,50€	13,00€	15,00€	34,50€
FC Kaiserslautern	12,00€	12,00€	17,00€	41,00€
TSV 1860 Munich	7,00€	14,00€	9,95€	36,00€
FC Erzgebirge Aue	12,00€	13,00€	22,00€	24,00€
FC St. Pauli	9,50€	14,50€	22,50€	43,00€
FC Union Berlin	11,00€	13,00€	28,00€	40,00€
Fortuna Düsseldorf	6,00€			38,00€
Eintracht Braun-schweig	11,00€	16,00€	7,00€	34,00€
Dynamo Dresden	13,50€	13,50€	18,00€	37,00€
SV Sandhausen	11,00€	13,00€	20,00€	28,00€
FC Heidenheim	3,00€	13,00€	7,00€	31,00€
Würzburger Kickers	12,00€	14,00€	22,00€	40,00€
Average	10,56€	13,13€	16,97€	37,11€